# Irresistible
# 1,2,3s

by Joan Novelli

## SCHOLASTIC
## PROFESSIONAL BOOKS

NEW YORK • TORONTO • LONDON • AUCKLAND • SYDNEY
MEXICO CITY • NEW DELHI • HONG KONG

*For my favorite young mathematicians:*
*Dylan, Elena, Sara, and Jonathan*

*Special thanks to the talented teachers who contributed ideas to this book:*
*Janet Bellevance, Nancy Cooper, Ann Flagg, Bob Krech,*
*Sue Lorey, Monica Lubic, Elaine Magud, Debbie Murphy, Mary Rosenberg,*
*Charlotte Sassman, Mary Beth Spann, and Natalie Vaughan.*

Cover design by Norma Ortiz
Cover art by John Wallace
Interior design by Solutions by Design, Inc.
Interior art by Liisa Chauncy Guida, except art on p. 20 by Shelley Dieterichs

"The End" by A. A. Milne. Reprinted from NOW WE ARE SIX by A. A. Milne.
Reprinted by permission of Dutton, a division of Penguin Putnam USA Inc.

"It All Adds Up" by Meish Goldish. Reprinted from *Thematic Songs and Fingerplays* by Meish Goldish.
Copyright © 1993 Scholastic Professional Books.

ISBN 0-439-04095-7

Copyright © 2000 by Joan Novelli
Printed in the U.S.A. All rights reserved.

# Contents

# About This Book

Numbers are a natural part of a child's earliest vocabulary. My young friend Zoe, just 18 months old, is already adding words for numbers to her vocabulary. "How many fingers?" "Two," she answers with confidence. For now, there are always two fingers, two blocks, two trucks, two toes, two books—whatever the actual number of objects. *Two* is an important part of Zoe's growing math vocabulary!

Learning to name, recognize, and write numbers forms a foundation for further understandings of mathematics. The *Curriculum and Evaluation Standards for School Mathematics* (NCTM) states that "the learning of mathematics must be an active process. Throughout the standards, such verbs as explore, justify, represent, solve, construct, discuss, use, investigate, describe, develop, and predict are used to convey this active physical and mental involvement of children in learning the content of the curriculum." This book is designed to help you engage children in active ways as they learn about numbers. Highlights include:

☼ **Teacher-Tested Ideas:** Many of the activities in this book come from classroom teachers across the country.

☼ **Multisensory Activities:** Your students will engage their senses with activities that invite them to listen, touch, see, and say. Kinesthetic activities invite them to learn through movement.

☼ **Reproducible Activity Pages:** Games, puzzles, templates, mini-books, and other ready-to-use pages reinforce number skills and concepts.

☼ **Building on Books:** Support students' learning with picture books. See Building on Books throughout for suggested titles and follow-up activities.

☼ **Poems and Fingerplays:** These rhymes enliven math lessons on numbers and provide lots of opportunities for related activities.

☼ **Interactive Displays:** Pocket chart activities, banners, and other colorful displays invite children to collaborate in the learning process.

☼ **Computer Connections:** Enhance your math program with award-winning software, teacher-tested web sites, and other technology tools.

☼ **Where to Learn More:** Find out about teacher resources for building a rich math program.

☼ **And Lots More!**

# Number Recognition and Counting

## Number Play

Set up a corner in your classroom for playing with numbers. Provide an assortment of materials for free play, such as:

- ☀ **Playing Cards:** Stock a basket with several sets of playing cards. Children will share games they know and create new ones, all the while looking at and learning about numbers.

- ☀ **Board Games:** Many board games involve rolling dice or using a spinner—in both cases counting spaces to move. Look at thrift stores and yard sales for games such as *Sorry!* and *Candyland*.

- ☀ **House Numbers:** Look for these in hardware and discount stores, in a variety of sizes, shapes, and colors. Children can sequence them, make number sentences with them, show their house number, show their age, show their room number, show their phone numbers, and so on.

- ☀ **Dice:** Fill a basket with dice in assorted sizes and colors. Children will create games to play with them. Check old games, as well as craft and toy stores, for spare dice.

- ☀ **Spinners:** Spinners from old board games make fun math manipulatives. Children can spin them to see how many spins it takes, for example, to get three fives. They'll make up their own games, too.

- ☀ **Phone Books and a Play Phone:** Young children will "look up" numbers in the phone book and dial them on the play phone. In time, they'll be looking up friends' numbers, the number for a favorite toy store, and so on.

Monica Lubic
Charlotte Elementary School
Charlotte, Vermont

### BUILDING ON BOOKS

***Count on Clifford***
by Norman Bridwell
(Scholastic, 1985)

Count along as Emily Elizabeth gets ready for her big red dog's birthday. A surprise ending shows Clifford saving the day as rain threatens to ruin the big event. Follow up by letting children plan their own imaginary birthday parties. *How many invitations? How many boys? How many girls?*

# Rainbow Number Books

Write each number from 1 to 10 on a sheet of paper for each child. Make the numbers big. Have children trace around the numbers several times using different colored crayons. Put children's pages together to make books. Let children read their number books aloud. They'll enjoy taking them home to read with their families, too.

Natalie Vaughan
Phoenix School
Encinitas, California

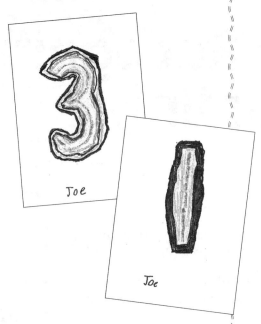

# Counting on Rabbits Number Wheel

Pair this activity with a reading of *Seven Little Rabbits* (see Building on Books, right) to reinforce counting skills. Give each child a copy of pages 16–17. Have children cut out the top and bottom wheels. Let children color in the rabbits if they like, then help them attach the wheels at the center with a paper fastener. Have children turn the wheel to count the rabbits. For a challenge, they can count how many rabbits there are all together.

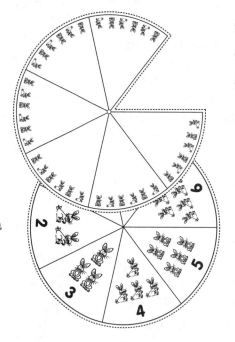

## Where to Learn More

*Turn to Learn* by Virginia Dooley (Scholastic Professional Books, 1996) includes reproducible wheels for teaching counting, number facts, and other math skills.

## BUILDING ON BOOKS

### *Seven Little Rabbits*

by John Becker
(Scholastic, 1973)

Young readers will enjoy chiming in on the rhyming words and repetitive text in this delightful counting book, illustrated by Caldecott Medal-winning Barbara Cooney. Let children take turns acting out the parts of the seven little rabbits as you read the story again and again.

# Number Basketball

Reinforce number recognition with a game that will become a favorite. Set up a wastepaper basket in an open space. Write the numbers you want to reinforce (or pictures that represent those numbers) on slips of paper. Lay them out on the floor about ten feet from the basket. Call out one of the numbers. Let children take turns coming up to find the number you call out, crumpling it up, and shooting it into the basket. Write enough numbers on the slips so that every child will be able to take at least a couple of shots. This is a fun activity for children to set up and play on their own—a variation that will provide practice in writing the numbers, too.

> Janet Bellevance
> Edmunds Elementary School
> Burlington, Vermont

# Who's My Match?

Play a movement matching game to strengthen number recognition and counting skills.

☀ Make a set of numeral cards for half of your students. For example, if you have 22 students, you'll need the numbers 1 to 11. (See page 18.)

☀ Copy and cut apart a set of picture cards to match the numeral cards. (See page 19.)

☀ String numeral and picture cards on yarn to make necklaces.

☀ Have students put their heads down and hold up one hand. Slip a necklace into each student's hand.

Children might like to color in their picture cards before playing the game. When you're ready to introduce concepts of number operations (see page 24), make necklaces that have matching number sentences—for example 3 + 3 and 1 + 5; 10 - 3 and 4 + 3; and 14 - 9 and 12 - 7. (Students find a match by locating a partner wearing a number sentence necklace with the same answer.)

☀ When you say "Go," have students raise their heads, put on their necklaces, then get up and try to find a classmate with a matching card.

☀ When everyone has a partner with a matching necklace, gather students together. Count the objects on each picture card. Compare the count to the matching numeral card.

> Debbie Murphy
> Richboro Elementary School
> Richboro, Pennsylvania

# Concentration

Use the number and picture cards on pages 18–19 for a game of Concentration. Copy each page and color and cut out the cards. Mix them up and place them facedown in rows and columns. Let children play with partners, taking turns flipping over two cards. If the cards match (number and picture), the player keeps the cards. If the cards do not match, the player turns them facedown. Make copies of the number and picture cards for children to take home. They can color and cut out the cards and play Concentration with their families. (Provide zipper-close bags to hold the cards.)

# Paper Pick-Up

Practice counting at the end of the day (or after an art project) with an activity that doubles as clean-up. When you say "Go!" have children pick up as many pieces of paper as they can find on the floor. After one minute, say "Stop!" and have children put the paper on their desks. Let each child count his or her own pieces. Do a class count, too. Have children count the pieces one by one, adding on to the last child's number. Pass around the wastebasket and admire your clean floor!

> Natalie Vaughan
> Phoenix School
> Encinitas, California

**COMPUTER CONNECTION**

The always popular *I Spy* series of books, puzzles, games, and more by Jean Marzollo and Walter Wick now includes the software *I Spy Junior* (Scholastic) for ages 3 to 5. Six riddle and game areas include activities to teach number recognition, counting, and other early math skills.

# 123 Race

Everyone's a winner in a cooperative race that reinforces number recognition and order. Children will have fun playing it again and again to beat the class time.

☀ Prepare for the race by making a set of number cards. Start with the number 1 and continue so that each child can have a card.

☀ Gather children in a circle. Mix up the cards and give one to each child. Explain that you are going to call out the numbers in order, starting with 1. When children hear their numbers, they need to hold up their cards over their heads. Tell students that you are going to time them to see how fast the class can get through all of the numbers in order.

☀ Call out the number 1 and wait for the child with that number to hold up his or her card. Continue calling the numbers in order, having each child hold up his or her card. Stop the clock when the child with the last number holds up that card.

☀ Talk about strategies for improving the class time then have another race. Can students work together to improve their time?

> Natalie Vaughan
> Phoenix School
> Encinitas, California

# I Spy Art

After sharing *I Spy Two Eyes* (see Building on Books, right), let children create their own I Spy pictures using the book as a model. Give children two sheets each of 8 1/2- by 11-inch paper. Have them create a picture on one sheet of paper, including any number of an object of their choice. On the second sheet of paper, have them complete this

## BUILDING ON BOOKS

**I Spy Two Eyes**
devised and selected by
Lucy Micklethwait
(Greenwillow, 1993)

Introduce children to fine art with this inviting counting book. They'll find one fly in *Portrait of a Woman of the Hofer Family*, two eyes in Karel Appel's *Cry for Freedom*, three puppies in Gauguin's *Still Life with Three Puppies*, four fish in Matisse's *Goldfish*, and more—right on up to 20 angels in Botticelli's *Mystic Nativity*.

sentence frame: *I spy _____ .* For example, if a child draws three children and a cat, he or she might write *I spy eight eyes*. Have children write the corresponding numeral beneath the sentence. Give each child a sheet of large construction paper. Have them glue their I Spy pictures and sentences side by side on the paper. Display the I Spy art, and give children time to find and count the objects in each picture.

## Pocket Count

How many pockets are students wearing all together? Finding the answer puts counting and problem-solving skills to work. Children never tire of this math game, and will even ask when they can play again so that they can plan on wearing outfits with lots of pockets on that day.

* Ask children to estimate how many pockets there are on their clothes that day. Have them record estimates.

* Give each child a handful of counters, such as dried beans. Ask children to place a counter in each pocket of their clothing.

* Bring children together in a circle and have them take all of the counters out of their pockets. Ask children to place their counters in the center of the circle.

* Let children take turns counting the dried beans into groups of ten. Count by tens to find a total.

* Invite children to tell how close they came with their estimates. Have them share their strategies for making estimates. For example, they might recognize that children wearing overalls will have lots of pockets, while children wearing sweatpants may have few.

Janet Bellevance
Edmunds Elementary
Burlington, Vermont

## BUILDING ON BOOKS

### *Feast for 10*
by Cathryn Falwell
(Scholastic, 1993)

It's off to the grocery store to shop for a feast: one cart, two pumpkins, three chickens, and more…enough for ten hungry guests. After sharing the story, count the items in the book: *How many are there all together?* As a follow-up, draw and cut out a big shopping-cart shape. Invite students to plan an imaginary feast. "Go shopping" for the foods. Let each child draw and cut out items to place in the cart. Count them!

# Grab Bag Math

Place a number of fun objects in a bag—for example, 20 marbles. How many will fit in a handful? Have students take turns grabbing a handful, then counting the objects. Have children record their names and totals on a chart. Compare results when everyone has taken a turn. *How many objects did most children fit in their hands? What was the range?* As you play the game with different objects, let students guess whether they will be able to hold the same amount, more, or less.

Use Grab Bag Math to reinforce other math skills.

☼ To practice subtraction, let children grab a handful of objects from the bag and count them. Have them tell how many are left in the bag.

☼ Let children play in pairs. Have one take a handful of objects and keep his or her hand closed. Have the other child count how many are left in the bag, then tell how many are hidden in the partner's hand.

# Birthday Pocket Chart Poem

A. A. Milne's poem "The End" is a favorite with young children, especially on their birthdays! Use it to teach number recognition, also to help children learn the words for numbers. To make a birthday pocket chart with the poem, write each line on a sentence strip. Copy and cut apart the picture and number cards on pages 18–19. Place the sentence strips and words in order on the chart. Place the picture and number cards to one side. Read the poem aloud with students. Reread it, letting children insert the number and picture-cards in the poem in place of the words *One, Two, Three, Four, Five,* and *Six.* Other ways to use the pocket chart follow.

☀ Let children match number and picture cards on the chart.

☀ Cut off the last word on each line. Place these word cards to one side of the pocket chart. Let children choose the words to complete each line.

☀ Cut up the sentence strips word by word. Let children help one another put the poem together in the pocket chart. (You may provide a copy of the complete poem as reference. See page 20.)

**COMPUTER CONNECTION**

From counting candles to cutting cake, birthdays are full of math fun. *Blue's Birthday Adventures* (Humongous Entertainment), for ages 3 to 6, invites children to play games and solve clues using an assortment of skills, including visual discrimination and counting.

☀ Give children copies of the poem on page 20. (White-out the number words on a copy first then make additional copies.) Let children complete the poem, filling in the numbers.

> Janet Bellevance
> Edmunds Elementary School
> Burlington, Vermont

### Where to Learn More

*The Great Big Book of Classroom Songs, Rhymes, and Cheers* by Ellen Booth Church (Scholastic Professional Books, 2000) includes a section on counting rhymes with teaching activities for enriching the experience.

## Ring in Math

Get students in the mood for math—and practice counting skills—by playing Ring in Math. When you're ready to begin a math lesson, ring a bell a distinct number of times. Let your students know that when they hear the bell, it's time to listen carefully and count. Those who are tuned in will be able to respond when you ask, "How many times did you hear the bell ring?"

> Ann Flagg
> Edu-Prize School
> Gilbert, Arizona

## Numbers and Names

Let children sort names by numbers of letters to reinforce counting skills. Set up the activity by dividing a sheet of oaktag into at least as many squares as the longest name on your class list. For example, if the longest name in your class is *Alexandria*, you would need at least ten squares. Write a

number on each square, starting with 1. Print students' names on small cards and place them in a basket near the number grid. Let children take turns, independently or in small groups, counting letters in names and placing them in the correct squares on the grid. Follow up by asking questions about the names and numbers—for example:

☀ Which number has the most name cards on it?

☀ Are there any number squares that don't have any names on them?

☀ How many names have fewer than eight letters? More than eight letters?

> Elaine Magud
> Joshua Cowell School
> Manteca, California

**TIP**

You can also set up Numbers and Names as a graph, as shown. Let children place the names in the correct columns.

| How many letters are in your name? | | | | | | | | | |
|---|---|---|---|---|---|---|---|---|---|
| 1 | 2 | 3 | 4 | 5 | 6 | 7 | 8 | 9 | 10 |
| T | a | n | i | s | h | a | | | |
| R | o | b | b | y | | | | | |
| E | v | a | | | | | | | |

# 101 Counting Jars

Gather 101 similar-sized jars. (Small baby-food jars work great.) With a permanent marker, label each jar with the numerals 0–100 (writing the numeral on the front, back, and top of the jar). Fill each jar with small beads (or a similar item), matching the number of beads with the numeral on the jar. Use the jars for a variety of activities, such as:

☀ Organize the jars in numerical order.

☀ Select the jars that represent the tens.

☀ Look for jars of a given number.

☀ Compare large and small collections.

> Charlotte Sassman
> Alice Carlson Applied Learning Center
> Fort Worth, Texas

**TIP**

When filling the jars, start at 100 to make sure the jar will hold this quantity.

# A Phone Book of Friends

Phone numbers become interesting to children in the early grades, when they begin to call friends all on their own—to make play dates or just to talk about a favorite toy. Use phone numbers to reinforce number recognition and help children see the ways people use mathematics in everyday life.

☀ Start by sending home a note requesting permission for students to share phone numbers in class.

☀ Make multiple copies of the phone number form on page 21. Model how to fill out the form.

☀ Invite children to use the forms to exchange phone numbers. They can record birthdays, too.

Keep the activity open-ended, placing the forms in an easily accessible place and letting students complete them as the need or interest arises. Or, make a class set for each child. (Write in children's names before photocopying.) Over a period of a week or two, let children circulate around the room, collecting phone numbers.

Mary Beth Spann
Education Consultant
Shoreham, New York

## BUILDING ON BOOKS

### One Hungry Monster
by Susan Hayboer O'Keefe
(Scholastic, 1989)

"One hungry monster underneath my bed, moaning and groaning and begging to be fed." Soon it's ten hungry monsters, and what they do with the food they're fed is everything children are not supposed to do—making this book all the more fun. Follow up by counting foods at lunchtime: *How many sandwiches? How many milks? How many apples? How many cookies?*

# Fishing for Numbers

Stock a "pond" with "fish" and let children go fishing for numbers! A wading pool makes a fun pond. You can also decorate a big cardboard box with blue paper. Make multiple copies of the fish on page 22. Write a number on each fish, then have children color in the fish and cut them out. Attach a paper clip to each fish and place it in the "pond." Make a fishing pole by tying string to a dowel. Tie a magnet to the end of the string. Let children use the fishing pole to catch fish, touching the magnet on the end of the string to the paper clip on a fish. They can simply count the number of fish they catch, read the numbers on the fish, or add up the numbers on the fish.

# I Spy a Number

Play this I Spy game to reinforce counting and number recognition skills.

☀ Begin by counting some number of objects in a group—for example, windows in the classroom. (Do not reveal what you are counting.) Say "I spy something that adds up to [the number]."

☀ Have children in the group respond with their guesses. When the answer is revealed, let the child who guessed correctly take a turn.

☀ Continue, letting a different child be the "I spy" counter each time.

# Numbers I Know

What numbers are important in your students' lives? Age is a big number for many children. They know how old they are and will gladly tell you old they'll be on their next birthday. Height and weight may be familiar numbers after a visit to the doctor. Then there are addresses, phone numbers, bus numbers, and so on. Children's lives are filled with numbers. The reproducible on page 23 lets them see just how many numbers they already know!

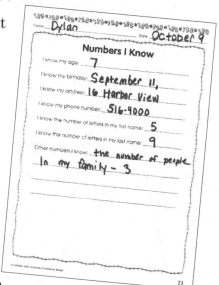

Copy a class set of page 23 and give one to each child. Read the sentences aloud with children. Have them fill in numbers they know, asking for help with numbers they're not sure of. For a challenge, graph some of the numbers children write down. For example, graph the class by age. Or, graph frequency of numbers in phone numbers. (*How many 1s, 2s, 3s, and so on?*)

You can play this I Spy game anywhere and anytime—for example, play while you're waiting in the lunch line. How many children are not wearing blue jeans? Count them and say "I spy (the number of children not wearing blue jeans)." Let children try to figure out what the number goes with. They'll stay busy and develop some flexible thinking skills, too!

# Counting On Rabbits

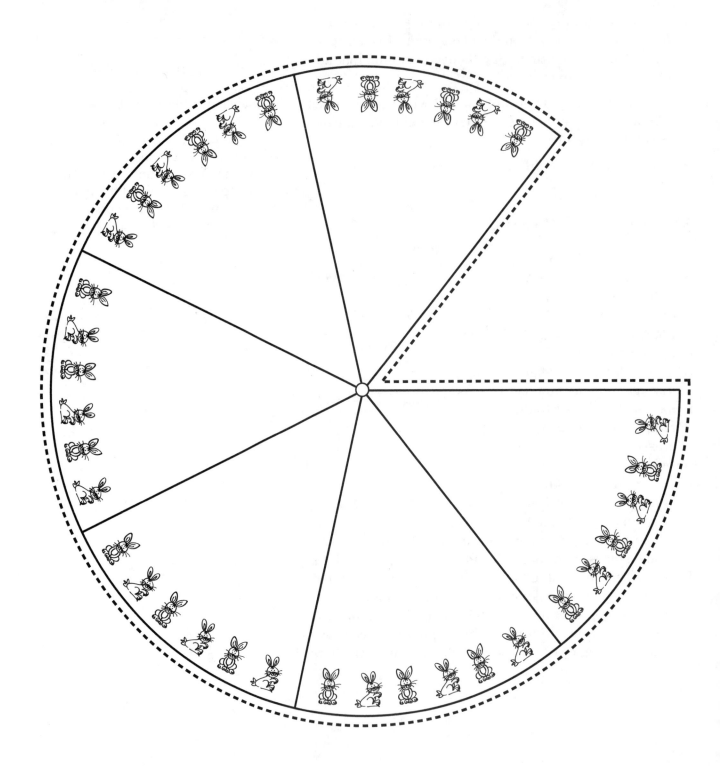

*Irresistible 123s* Scholastic Professional Books

# Counting On Rabbits

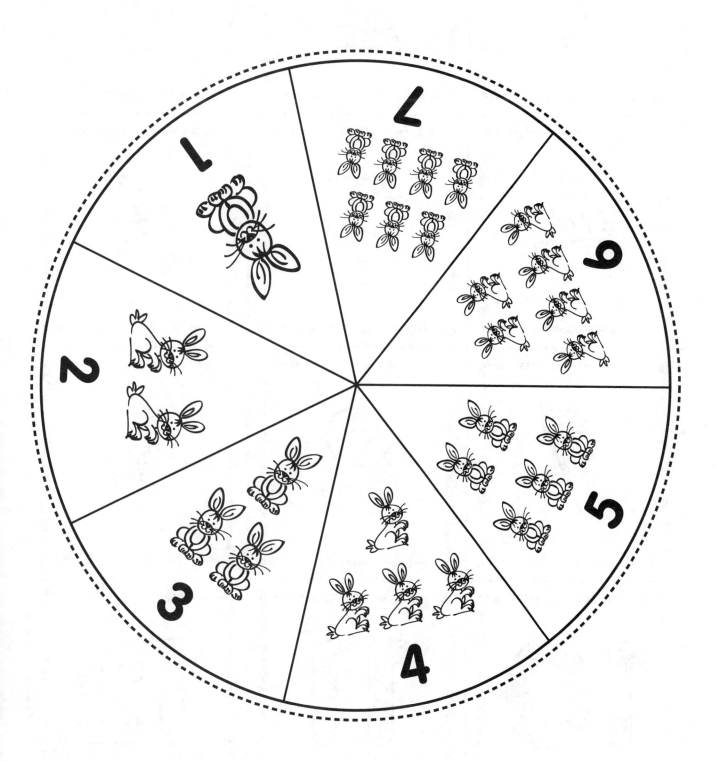

18

Name _____   Date _____

# The End

When I was One,
I had just begun.
When I was Two,
I was nearly new.
When I was Three,
I was hardly me.
When I was Four,
I was not much more.
When I was Five,
I was just alive.
But now I'm Six, I'm as clever as clever,
So I think I'll be six now for ever and ever.
　—A. A. Milne

## TRY THIS!

❋ Find the number words in the poem.
Circle them!

❋ Draw a birthday cake on the back
of this paper. Color candles to show
how many years old you are.

"The End" by A. A. Milne. Reprinted from NOW WE ARE SIX by A. A. Milne. Reprinted by permission of Dutton, a division of Penguin Putnam USA Inc.

Name _____  Date _____

# A Phone Book of Friends

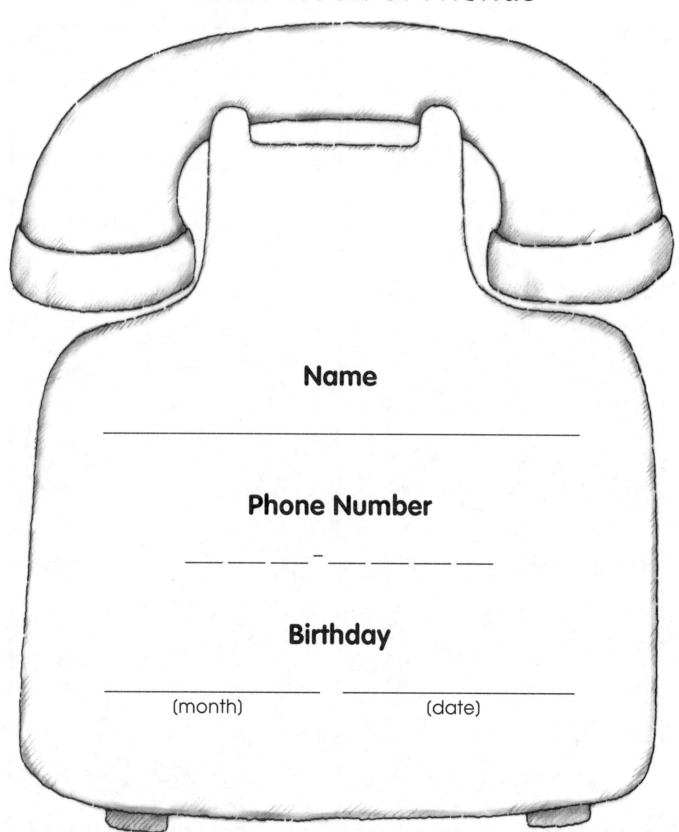

**Name**

_____

**Phone Number**

___ ___ ___ — ___ ___ ___ ___

**Birthday**

_____  _____

(month)                          (date)

Name _____ Date _____

# Fishing for Numbers

*Irresistible 123s* Scholastic Professional Books

Name _____  Date _____

# Numbers I Know

I know my age: _____

I know my birthday: _____

I know my address: _____

I know my phone number: _____

I know the number of letters in my first name: _____

I know the number of letters in my last name: _____

Other numbers I know: _____

_____

_____

_____

# Number Concepts

## Question of the Day

Help children identify quantities, recognize relationships between numbers, and begin to learn about addition and subtraction with a Question of the Day. Post a number concepts question before children come into the room each day. Have students write answers on slips of paper and place them in a Question of the Day box. (Younger children may want to dictate their answers to you.) Set aside time at the end of the day to reveal the answer. Encourage flexible thinking by letting children share their reasoning behind possible answers. Discuss the different ways of finding an answer to the question. Sample questions follow.

☼ If we need to pair up for an activity today, will each child have a partner?

☼ If the children in our class share 12 cupcakes, will we have enough if we cut them in half?

> Monica Lubic
> Charlotte Elementary School
> Charlotte, Vermont

## If Numbers Could Talk

Help children discover the ways numbers give information with this sentence-completion activity.

☼ Invite children to look around the classroom. Ask: *What numbers do you see?*

☼ Write this sentence frame on the chalkboard: *The number _____ tells me _____ .* Have children complete the sentence—for example, *The number 6 tells me how many candles will be on my next birthday cake.*

☼ Write the sentence frame on paper and copy a class set. Have children complete the sentence and illustrate it. Put the pages together to make a class book.

> Sue Lorey
> Grove Avenue School
> Barrington, Illinois

This activity makes a great homework assignment. Have children copy the sentence frame and take it home. Have them complete it for numbers they see at home—for example, on VCRs and TVs, on price tags, on cereal boxes, on clothing tags, and so on.

# Ordinal Number Calendar Activity

Teach ordinal number concepts with a daily calendar activity. Hide surprises under flaps on a wall calendar. (You can use sticky-notes.) Each day, use an ordinal number to tell children where the surprise is hidden. For example, say, "Look for a sticker under the seventh square." Other surprises you can hide include jokes and riddles, fun facts about the day, a special class treat such as an extra recess, and so on. (For a literature connection, see Building on Books, right.)

> Debbie Murphy
> Richboro Elementary School
> Richboro, Pennsylvania

# We're Going on a Field Trip!

The next time your class is planning a field trip, use the opportunity to reinforce number concepts. (You can plan an imaginary field trip, too, for the same results.) From the beginning, look for situations that will let children apply math skills. Examples follow.

❋ When permission slips start coming in, ask: *How many have been returned? How many still need to be returned?*

❋ If you're traveling by car, ask students how many cars they think the class will need to transport everyone. If each car holds three children, how many cars will the class need?

❋ Mark the field trip date on the calendar. Each day, have students find out how many days until the field trip.

## BUILDING ON BOOKS

### *Seven Blind Mice*
by Ed Young
(Philomel, 1992)

This Caldecott Honor book reinforces concepts of ordinal numbers as seven blind mice investigate something strange in their pond. The Red Mouse is first to venture out to solve the mystery. The Green Mouse is second, the Yellow Mouse third, and so on. Each mouse sees only a part of the strange "something," until finally the seventh mouse puts the pieces together. This is also a wonderful story for teaching parts of a whole. As the story says, "Knowing in part may make a fine tale, but wisdom comes from seeing the whole."

# Who Goes Next?

When teaching students about ordering numbers, play "Who Goes Next?" to provide practice.

☀ Make and laminate a number card for each child. For example, if you have 22 students, make and laminate cards with the numbers 1-22.

☀ Ask students to put their heads down and hold up one hand.

☀ Slip a number card into each student's hand. Then say "Heads up," and let students look at their cards.

☀ Have students then work together to put themselves in numerical order. (You can write the word FIRST on the chalkboard to give students a place to start lining up.) This is a great way to teach number order and to foster communication and cooperation in the classroom.

> Debbie Murphy
> Richboro Elementary School
> Richboro, Pennsylvania

# Number Match

Use blank index cards to make number games that support other areas of your curriculum. For example, if you're learning about insects in science, make a "Creepy Crawly Matching Game."

☀ Make a set of insect counting cards by gluing pictures of insects representing the numbers one to ten on index cards. (Glue one insect picture on a card, two on another card, three on a third card, and so on.) Make two sets of these picture cards.

☀ Write the numerals 1 to 10 on index cards.

☀ Write the words *one* to *ten* on index cards.

☀ To play, have children turn the cards facedown, then take turns flipping two cards over to try and make a match. They can match numeral and picture cards, and picture and word cards. This is a great way to reinforce number concepts thematically. Vary the game to cover any other topic, such as sea life, pond animals, and plants.

> Nancy Cooper
> Mabel I. Wilson School
> Cumberland, Maine

## BUILDING ON BOOKS

### *The Right Number of Elephants*

by Jeff Sheppard
(Scholastic, 1990)

Share this favorite story to practice counting backward from 10 to 1. Then let children count backward using themselves as counters. Start by lining them up. Have a child at one end begin the countdown—starting with the number of children in the line. Have each child sit as he or she says the next number. Continue until you reach the last student standing (the number "1" child). After that child sits, ask: *How many standing?* (zero or none)

26

# Collaborative Classroom Banner

This collaborative banner encourages children to think about numbers in new ways. To make the banner, give each child a copy of page 31. Show children how to cut along the dashed lines to make the door. Have children spread glue on the back of the paper (avoiding the door area) and place it glue-side down on construction paper. To complete the banner, ask children to think of a favorite number and write a riddle about that number in the space provided. For example, a child whose favorite number is three might write, "I am two more than one and three less than six." Have children write their favorite numbers inside the door.

To make the banner, have children tape their riddles together side to side. (Or, cut craft paper to size and staple or glue banner pages side to side.) Display on a wall and let children try to guess one another's favorite numbers.

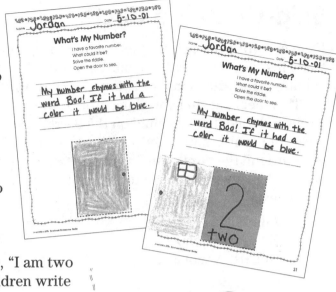

# Number Jump

This game gives children practice sequencing the numbers 1 to 10. (You can adapt it to sequence any series of numbers.) To make the game board, divide a sentence strip into 11 sections. Cut up another sentence strip into 11 equal pieces. Write the numbers 1 to 10 on the pieces. Discard the extra piece. Set up the game by placing the numbers in random order on the sentence-strip game board. Model with a volunteer how to play. Take turns moving the pieces by jumping over a number into an empty space or by sliding "next door" (left or right) to an empty space. Continue taking turns until all of the numbers are in order.

Mary Rosenberg
Kratt Elementary School
Fresno, California

## TIP

To make this game more challenging, ask students to try to put the numbers in order without talking to one another.

## BUILDING ON BOOKS

**Ten, Nine, Eight**
by Molly Bang
(Greenwillow, 1983)

From "ten small toes all washed and warm" to "1 big girl all ready for bed," this book uses sets of objects to count down to bedtime. Give children cards on which you've written the numbers 1 to 10. (Or use the reproducible number cards on page 18.) Let children hold up the matching numbers as you read the story. Then retell the story, letting children suggest new sets for the numbers 1 to 10.

27

# Skip-Counting Circle

Keep everyone on their toes as you practice counting by twos, fives, or tens. Gather children in a circle. Practice counting from the number of your choice to warm everyone up. Then begin again by walking around the outside of the circle and touching one child on the head. When the child feels your touch, have him begin the sequence. Continue to walk around the circle, quickly touching children at random and giving them a turn to say the number that would come next.

> Ann Flagg
> Edu-Prize School
> Gilbert, Arizona

# Mystery Number Game

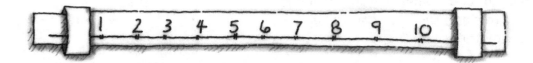

*What's my mystery number?* Children love guessing games, especially when they involve using clues to find an answer. Play this mystery number game with the class often to strengthen number concepts. Children can play it on their own, too.

☀ Make a number line by writing the numbers 1–10 (or any other range) on a strip of tagboard. Make two "sliders" by cutting small strips of tagboard and taping the ends together to form loops. Place the sliders over each end of the number line. Tack up the number line.

☀ Tell children that you are thinking of a number between one and ten (or any other range). Invite them to take turns guessing the mystery number. If they guess a number that is low, move the slider on the left to that number to indicate that the mystery number is higher. If they guess a number that is high, move the slider on the right to that number to indicate that the mystery number is lower. In this way, students narrow down the range to see which two numbers the mystery number is between.

> Monica Lubic
> Charlotte Elementary School
> Charlotte, Vermont

28

# Spill the Bag

Strengthen number sense with an activity that lets children match sets of objects to number cards.

☀ Fill a bag with sets of objects—for example, one toy car, two marbles, three erasers, four dice, five crayons, and so on.

☀ Make number cards to go with the sets. (You may write just the numeral on these cards or both the numeral and number word.)

☀ Place the bag at a learning center. Let children visit independently or with partners to spill the bag and match objects to number cards.

☀ Change the objects from day to day to keep the activity fresh and to teach new numbers.

> Natalie Vaughan
> Phoenix School
> Encinitas, California

# Rainy Day Math

When the weather keeps your students indoors for recess, try this activity. Students love it, and it really reinforces number concepts and builds number sense.

☀ Gather lots of magazines.

☀ Pair up students, then give them several magazines and a piece of construction paper on which you've written a numeral and also the word—for example, *2* and *two*.

☀ Ask students to look through their magazines to find things that come in twos (or whatever their number is). Have them cut out the pictures (or words) that represent their number and glue them to the construction paper.

> Nancy Cooper
> Mabel I. Wilson School
> Cumberland, Maine

# Big and Small Numbers

This game invites children to think about numbers in different ways. Distribute two index cards to each student. Assign each student a number. Use a variety of numbers that you would like students to think about. Have students write their assigned numbers on their cards.

Ask students to think about ways their numbers can be big. Ask them to think about how their numbers can be small. Tell them they're going to write a sentence for each on their cards. Model the activity with your own number—for example:

*I have two white cards here. I'm going to write the number 10 on each card. That's my assigned number. Now, sometimes 10 can be a big number and sometimes it can be a small number. I'm going to write a sentence on each card with the number 10 in it. On one card I'm going tell how 10 might be a big number. On the other I'm going to write a sentence about how 10 might be a small number.*

Write your examples on the cards and share them with the class. Have students write sentences on their cards for their numbers. They can illustrate them, too, then share them with the class.

Bob Krech
Dutch Neck School
Princeton Junction, New Jersey

10 is a big number when it is the number of ice cream cones I eat.

10 is a small number when it is the number of hairs on your head.

# Big Number Fun Interactive Display

The extra-large numbers that fill this interactive display invite children to explore numbers on many levels.

☀ Cover a bulletin board with craft paper. Cut out the numbers 1–10 from oaktag. Let children use these as templates to trace and cut out more numbers. They can decorate the numbers with markers, adding stripes, polka dots, squiggly lines, and so on. Punch a hole at the top of each number. Use a straight pin to attach the stack of each number to the board.

☀ Let two children each take a number. Ask: *What numbers can you make by putting your numbers together?* Let them arrange themselves to form the numbers. Try three and four digit numbers, too.

☀ Take a number walk. Have children each select a number from the board, then walk around the classroom (or to some destination in the school) trying to find that number somewhere else.

☀ Give 10 children one number each (from 1 to 10), and have them arrange themselves in numerical order.

☀ Give children numbers. Let them sort themselves by odd and even numbers.

Name _____     Date _____

# What's My Number?

I have a favorite number.
What could it be?
Solve the riddle.
Open the door to see.

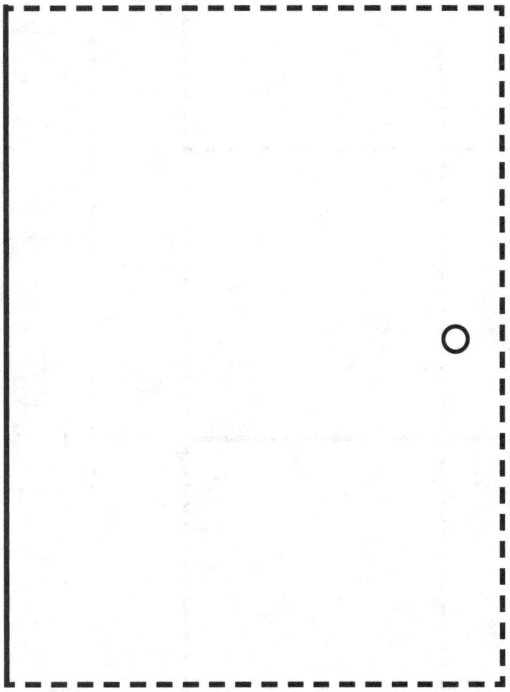

_____

_____

_____

_____

_____

# Number Jump

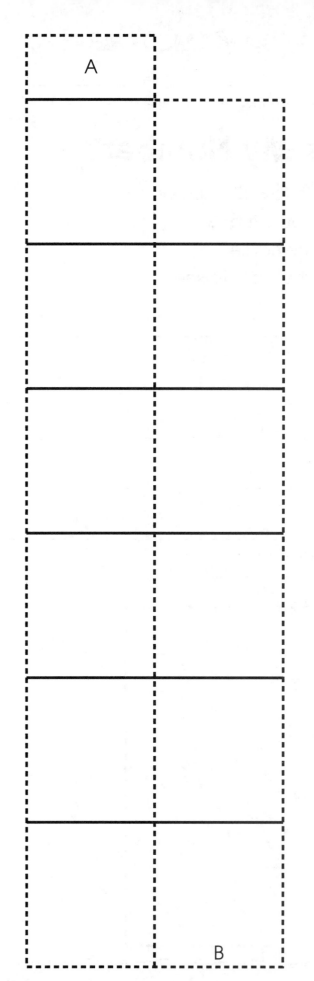

A

B

*Irresistible 123s* Scholastic Professional Books

# Concepts of Number Operations

## Operation!

When young children are learning about mathematical operations, many of them perform addition no matter what the sign. This lesson will give them a reason to remember the difference between operations they're learning.

Tell students that they're going to have a visitor named "Dr. Math." Later in the day (after lunch or a special, for example), surprise your class by wearing surgical gloves and a surgical mask. Lower the mask and introduce yourself as Dr. Math. Tell students that you're here today to discuss operations. Share the following information as you prepare for the "operation."

☀ There are four operations: addition, subtraction, multiplication, and division. Show the symbol for each.

☀ Sometimes students forget to look to see what operation they are performing.

☀ Just like a surgeon has to check a patient's chart to see what type of operation is to be performed, students need to check their math problems to see what operation they are to perform.

Invite questions, then explain that you have a very busy schedule and are needed in surgery. As you leave the room, ham it up and yell, "I'm off to perform another operation!"

Nancy Cooper
Mabel I. Wilson School
Cumberland, Maine

## Number Hop

Big numbers on the floor invite children to move and do math. Set up the activity by writing the numbers 1 to 9 on oaktag squares and taping them securely to the floor to make a 3 by 3 grid. You can arrange the numbers in

### COMPUTER CONNECTION

Teach essential math skills with Davidson's Blaster series. For preschool through first grade, there's *Math Blaster, Jr.* Designed to allow children to progress through several levels of difficulty, this engaging software teaches beginning math and thinking skills, including identifying numbers and quantities, counting, and addition and subtraction.

sequence or in random order. Vary the game depending on the concepts you wish to strengthen. Suggestions follow:

* As a warm-up, challenge children to hop on each number in order—forward and backward.

* Pose a math problem—for example, 3 + 4. Have children hop to the answer on one foot, then land on the answer on both feet. Or, give the sum (such as 10) and have children hop on two numbers that add up to that number (such as 4 and 6).

* Let one child hop on one foot to as many numbers as he or she can while a partner records those numbers. Stop when the child touches down on both feet or touches a line. Add up the numbers.

## Clean-Up Math

At end of the day (or anytime), place detergent or shaving cream on kids' desks. Call out a math problem, then let children write a solution on their desks. Add water if the soap hardens. When you're ready to clean up, pass around a few rags, and let children wipe their desks clean!

## BUILDING ON BOOKS

### *Ten Black Dots*

by Donald Crews
(Scholastic, 1968)

What can one dot make? How about two dots? Students discover all sorts of possibilities in this classic counting book. After sharing the story, ask: *What other things can you do with one dot? two? three?* and so on. For a challenge, ask children how many black dots there are in all in the story. Let children discuss ways to find out, then calculate an answer. Follow up by having children make their own *Ten Black Dots* books. They'll have fun using round black stickers for the dots. (Check office supply stores.)

# Five Little Monkeys

Use a traditional fingerplay to reinforce counting and number operations. Give each child a copy of the fingerplay and the pattern page. (See pages 42–43.) Have children cut out and color the tree, crocodile, and monkeys. Have them glue the tree to a sheet of construction paper. Read aloud the rhyme, inviting children to use the crocodile and monkeys to act it out. They can begin by placing five monkeys in the tree. On the word "Snap!" what happens? (*One monkey disappears from the tree.*) Let students revisit the fingerplay, writing number sentences to show what happens in each verse.

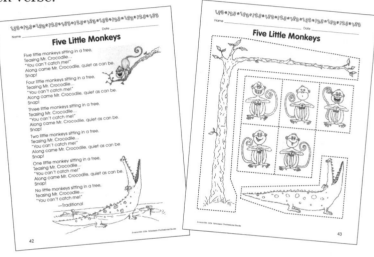

## *Where to Learn More*

*Math for the Very Young* by Lydia Polonsky et al. (John Wiley, 1995) is full of games, activities, songs, crafts, and other ideas for exploring math skills and concepts with young children. It includes a section on counting rhymes and stories.

# Counting With Cups

Place five small objects in a colorful opaque cup. Have a volunteer come up and count one, two, or three more objects. Ask: *How many objects are in the cup now?* Children will have to add in their heads to figure it out. Let them share answers, then dump out the contents of the cup and count together. Try the same game to practice subtraction, but have a child reach into the cup and take away a number of objects. Dump and count to check the answer.

Ann Flagg
Edu-Prize School
Gilbert, Arizona

## COMPUTER CONNECTION

For more number fingerplays, check these web sites:

www.preschoolrainbow.org/preschool-rhymes.htm

www.proteacher.com/020010.shtml

## BUILDING ON BOOKS
### *One Gorilla*
by Atsuko Morozumi
(Farrar, Straus & Giroux, 1990)

"Here is a list of things I love…" begins this lushly illustrated counting book. The list grows with one gorilla, two butterflies, three budgerigars, and so on. Use the story as a counting book, also as a springboard for problem solving—for example, ask: *How many things does the author love? How many things with four legs does the author love?* Let children do the math and share explanations for their answers.

# Bean Toss

Give each child a copy of the game board on page 44 and a handful of beans. Then guide children in playing a game to strengthen addition skills.

☀ One at a time, toss beans on your game board. (You might have students count out ten beans to toss.)

☀ Record the numbers on the spaces where the beans land. Add up the numbers. Play again. Try to get a higher total. Play again. Try to get a lower total.

# Moose Math

Here's a way to practice math facts, but it's a lot more fun than flash cards!

☀ Ask a student who is familiar with the card game "War" to explain how to play. Tell students that this card game is just a little bit different. Give each child a deck of cards and have them take out the Jacks, Queens, and Kings.

☀ Have students pair up to play: Both students turn over one card. Each card is the value of the number on it. The first student to add up the sum of the two numbers and say the answer gets to take the two cards. For example, if Sara turns over a three and Dylan turns over a five, the first one to say *eight* takes the cards.

☀ Students continue playing until both say the answer at the same time or both turn over the same number. Then they both yell MOOSE and place three cards facedown, then turn the next card over. Whoever is first to say the new sum takes all ten cards.

Nancy Cooper
Mabel I. Wilson School
Cumberland, Maine

Once students know their 1–10 facts well, add in the Jack, Queen, and King. (Jack = 11, Queen = 12, King = 13)

# Family Portraits

Pictures add up in these unique family portraits. Explain that before the alphabet and numbers, people used simple pictures, or *hieroglyphs*, to share information. Let your students make their own hieroglyphs to create portraits of their families.

Start by modeling the activity. Make a key, using simple pictures to stand for people and pets in your family. Record the key on chart paper or the chalkboard. (See samples below.) Using the key, make a portrait of your family, putting only one type of each family member (women, men, boys, girls, dogs, fish, and so on) on a line. Invite children to add with you as you count up family members in your picture. Write a math sentence to go with your picture.

Have children make their own keys (remind them to keep the pictures simple) and family portraits. Let them use addition signs to turn their portraits into math problems. Display family portraits, and let students add up one another's pictures. If your class is up to the challenge, try adding up a class total. You may want to have each child take a counter for every family member he or she pictured. Bring children together to group counters by ten. Count by tens for a class total.

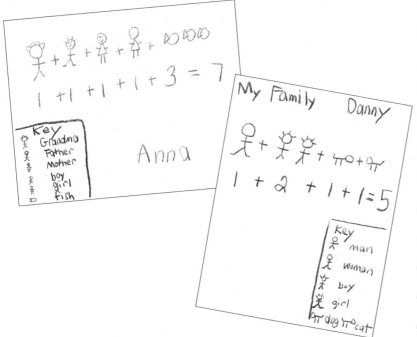

## Where to Learn More

Family Portraits is adapted from *Easy MathART: Projects and Activities* by Cecilia Dinio-Durkin (Scholastic Professional Books, 1999).

For a look that resembles the bark or animal skins people painted on long ago, try having children create their family portraits on brown paper grocery bags. Open them up and cut off the bottoms first.

# "It All Adds Up"
# Pocket Chart Poem

Copy the poem "It All Adds Up" (see page 45) on sentence strips. Snip off the last word of lines 2, 4, 6, 8, 10, 12, 14, 16, 18, and 20 to make number cards. Place the sentence strips in the pocket chart. Insert the number cards where they belong to make the poem complete. Read the poem aloud to children. Reread it, inviting them to chime in on the rhyming words. Set the number cards aside and read the poem a third time. Let children take turns choosing a number card to complete each sentence as you read the poem aloud again. Try these suggestions to extend the activity.

As you reread the poem "It All Adds Up" with students, vary the approach to keep interest high— for example, ask students to whisper the poem but shout the number words, sing the poem, clap the beats, say it slow, say it fast, and so on.

☀ Give children cards the size of the number cards (or a little bigger). Invite them to illustrate any one of the sentences in the poem by drawing a picture of that many children. Be sure at least one child illustrates each line. Place pictures in the pocket chart. Reread the poem, letting children complete it rebus-style with their picture cards.

☀ Place the pocket chart poem at a center where children can play with the poem independently or with a partner. They can use the number cards to complete the poem, match number and picture cards, and so on.

☀ Give each child a copy of the poem. Have children circle the number words, underline rhyming words, and so on.

☀ Give each child a copy of the picture page. (See page 46.) Have children color in the kids, cut them out, and arrange them in sets to show different ways to make ten. For example, they might place four friends in one group and six in another. Have children write number sentences to go with each combination. How many different ways can they make ten?

# Number Combination Mini-Books

Teach flexibility in thinking with number combination mini-books. Make a set of mini-books by cutting sheets of copy paper in half and stapling them together. Let children use the books to show how many ways they can make a number. For example, a child making a book about the number 4 may fill the pages with $0 + 4$, $10 - 6$, $0 + 0 + 0 + 0 + 4$, $2 + 2$, $100 - 96$, and so on. Let children take turns being the Calculator Checker, and checking their classmates' number combinations to see if they work.

> Janet Bellevance
> Edmunds Elementary School
> Burlington, Vermont

# Ring Around Math

Children can play this arcade-like game to build counting and addition skills.

☀ Fill five large soda bottles with water and cap tightly. Label the bottles one to five. Stagger the bottles, with one being closest and five furthest away. Use masking tape to mark a line a couple of yards from the closest bottle. Gather several rubber rings. (You might see if the physical education teacher has some you can borrow, find them in a toy store, or use large rubber seals for canning jars.)

☀ Have children take turns tossing a ring on a bottle. Record the number for each ring students get on a bottle. Add up the numbers to get a class score. Play again. Try for a higher score!

## COMPUTER CONNECTION

Children will have fun using the popular rubber stamps in *Kid Pix* (Broderbund) to create their number combination books. They can use the text tool to type the number sentences, and the rubber stamp tool to show the combination with pictures.

Discuss strategies for getting the highest score. For example, students might shoot for the bottles in the back. With a higher score per bottle (4 or 5), they may get a higher total score. Other students might figure that they have a better chance of getting their rings around a closer bottle. More rings around bottles may mean a higher score.

# How Many Hands?

As students count hands in the classroom, what will they learn? Whether they count by ones or twos, they can discover a pattern: one child, two hands; two children, four hands; three children, six hands; and so on. Write a number sentence to show how many hands there are. (2 + 2 + 2 + 2 + 2…) This activity also lays a foundation for multiplication (1 x 2 = 2; 2 x 2 = 4; 3 x 2 = 6; and so on).

# Hand Stamp Graph

Learn more about counting and number operations with a graph that lets children stamp their hands to record information. Set up a two-column graph. Label one "Right-Handed" and the other "Left-Handed." (You may also include a column for "Ambidextrous" if this applies to anyone in your class.) Give children copies of page 47 and have them cut apart and tape together the three sections to make individual graphs. Pour tempera paint into two paper plates. (Choose a different color for each column.) One at a time, have children lightly place one hand palm-side down in the correct color paint. Have the child then make a hand print in the correct column to show if he or she is left- or right-handed. Children can color in hands on their own graphs as each child stamps his or her hand print on the class graph. When the graph is complete, ask questions to guide a discussion—for example:

☀ *How many children are left-handed? right-handed?*

☀ *How many more children are [left- or right-handed] than [left- or right-handed]?*

## BUILDING ON BOOKS

### *Bat Jamboree*
by Kathi Appett
(Scholastic, 1996)

It's "standing room only" for the bat jamboree, performed each year by 55 bats. One bat sings, two flap, three cha-cha-cha, four tap. There are cartwheels, bat flips, and more—all leading up to the much-anticipated finale, when the "bat lady sings." Follow up by letting students solve math problems based on the story. For example:

☼ *Seven bats balanced seven balls and nine bats fluttered. How many bats balanced and fluttered?*

☼ *One bat sang. Four bats tapped. How many more bats tapped than sang?*

# Popcorn Adding Boards

With a handful of pop-
corn and a number cube,
children make adding
boards to practice num-
ber operations.

☀ Give each child a
handful of popcorn
kernels, a copy of
the adding board on
page 48, and a num-
ber cube.

☀ Let children roll
the number cube
and glue the corre-
sponding number
of popcorn ker-
nels in the first
square of number 1.

☀ Have children roll the number cube a second time, then
glue that number of popcorn kernels to the second
square of number 1.

☀ Have them add the two groups of kernels, then glue popcorn kernels in the third square (after the = sign) to
show the sum. Children can write the corresponding
number sentences underneath the popcorn equation.

☀ Have children continue to make more popcorn addition
sentences. Let them share their adding boards with one
another, reading the number sentences aloud.

> Natalie Vaughan
> Phoenix School
> Encinitas, California

## COMPUTER CONNECTION

*I'm Ready for
Kindergarten:
Huggly's Sleepover* (Scholastic) is
a skill-building adventure that
invites children ages 4 to 6 to join
a group of lovable monsters at a
sleepover. Children (and
monsters) put a range of math
and other skills to work as they
prepare for the party.

Name _____ Date _____

# Five Little Monkeys

Five little monkeys sitting in a tree,
Teasing Mr. Crocodile…
"You can't catch me!"
Along came Mr. Crocodile, quiet as can be.
Snap!

Four little monkeys sitting in a tree,
Teasing Mr. Crocodile…
"You can't catch me!"
Along came Mr. Crocodile, quiet as can be.
Snap!

Three little monkeys sitting in a tree,
Teasing Mr. Crocodile…
"You can't catch me!"
Along came Mr. Crocodile, quiet as can be.
Snap!

Two little monkeys sitting in a tree,
Teasing Mr. Crocodile…
"You can't catch me!"
Along came Mr. Crocodile, quiet as can be.
Snap!

One little monkey sitting in a tree,
Teasing Mr. Crocodile…
"You can't catch me!"
Along came Mr. Crocodile, quiet as can be.
Snap!

No little monkeys sitting in a tree,
Teasing Mr. Crocodile…
"You can't catch me!"

—Traditional

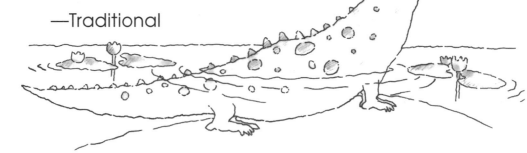

42

Name _____  Date _____

# Five Little Monkeys

Name _____ Date _____

# Bean Toss

Name _____  Date _____

# It All Adds Up

Once there was a lonely son,
Sad 'cause he was only one.

Then along came Cindy Lou,
Now they were a happy two!

Next they met Joanne Marie,
That made them a happy three!

Then along came Salvador,
Now they were a happy four!

Soon they saw Roberto Clive,
That made them a happy five!

They went to the house of Nick's,
Where they were a happy six!

Then along came Kenneth Kevin,
That made them a happy seven!

Next they met Melissa Kate,
Now they were a happy eight!

Then along came Caroline,
That made them a happy nine!

Finally they all met Gwen,
Ending up a happy ten!

—by Meish Goldish

---

**TRY THIS!** Underline the words in the poem that rhyme with the numbers *one, two, three, four, five, six, seven, eight, nine,* and *ten.*

---

# It All Adds Up

Name _____  Date _____

# Hand Stamp Graph

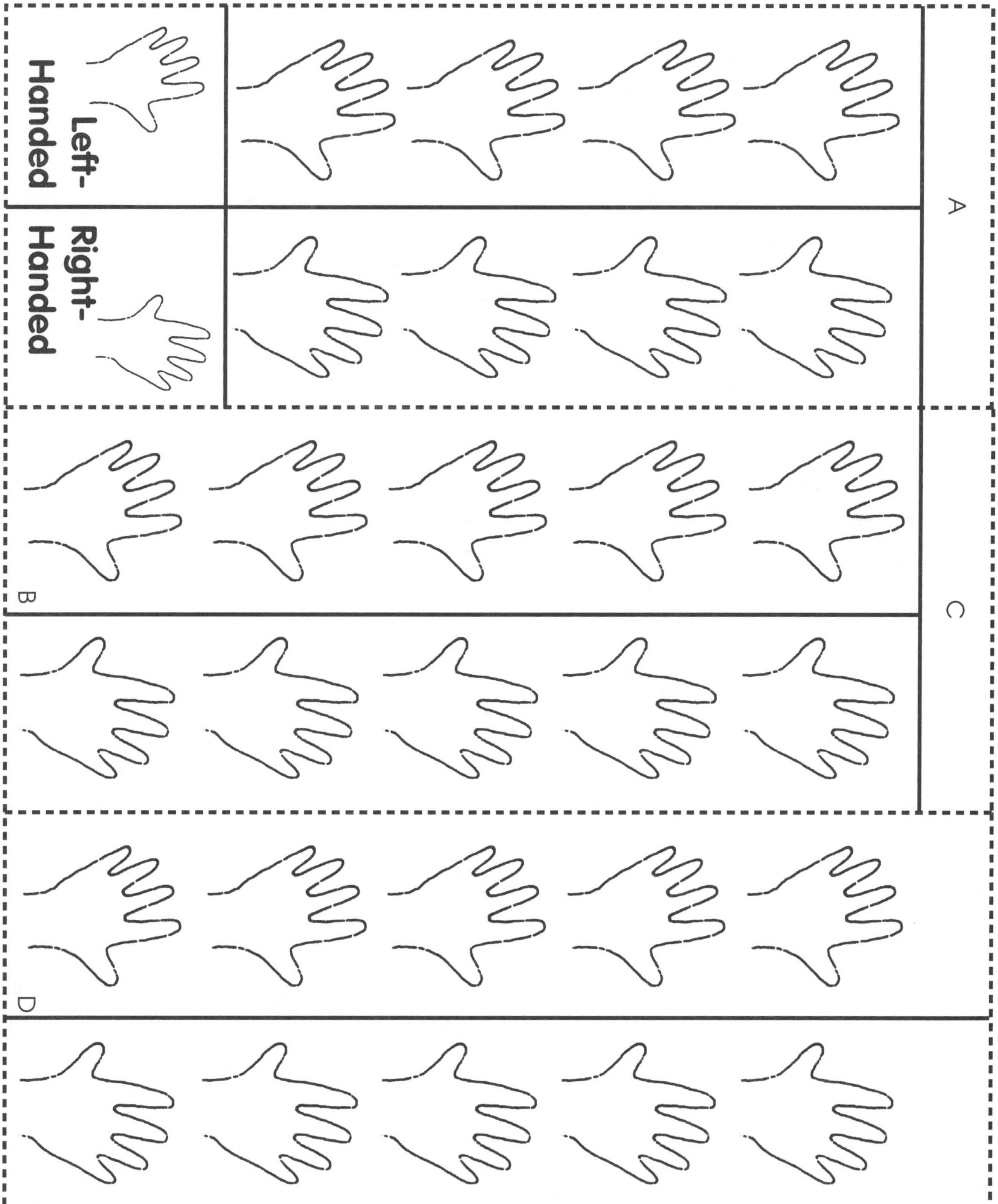

| Left-Handed | A |
|---|---|
| Right-Handed | |

B

C

D

Name _____  Date _____

# Popcorn Adding Board

1. ☐ + ☐ = ☐

_____ + _____ = _____

2. ☐ + ☐ = ☐

_____ + _____ = _____

3. ☐ + ☐ = ☐

_____ + _____ = _____

4. ☐ + ☐ = ☐

_____ + _____ = _____

*Irresistible 123s* Scholastic Professional Books